CW00683905

Charles Brasch

SELECTED POEMS

Charles Brasch

SELECTED POEMS

Chosen by

ALAN RODDICK

OTAGO UNIVERSITY PRESS

Published by Otago University Press
Level 1, 398 Cumberland Street
Dunedin, New Zealand
university.press@otago.ac.nz
www.otago.ac.nz/press

First published 2015

Copyright © The Estate of Charles Brasch
Introduction copyright © Alan Roddick

The moral rights of the authors have been asserted.

ISBN 978-1-877578-05-2

Published with the assistance of Creative New Zealand

A catalogue record for this book is available from the National Library of New Zealand.
This book is copyright. Except for the purpose of fair review, no part may be stored or
transmitted in any form or by any means, electronic or mechanical, including recording
or storage in any information retrieval system, without permission in writing from the
publishers. No reproduction may be made, whether by photocopying or by any other
means, unless a licence has been obtained from the publisher.

Cover painting: Max Gimblett, *In the Beginning was the Word and the Word Became Flesh
and Dwelt Among Us*, 2011. Gesso, acrylic & vinyl polymers, resin, water-based size,
23.75kt Swiss gold leaf/canvas. 2438 x 2032 x 51 mm (96 x 80 in.) Courtesy of the artist.

Printed in China through Asia Pacific Offset Ltd

CONTENTS

INTRODUCTION

CHARLES BRASCH'S POETRY collections may be long out of print, but his poems continue to be printed in anthologies, appear in novels as well as literary and social histories, and even inspire musical settings. The 2013 publication of his *Journals 1939–1945* has renewed interest in his life and work. For this *Selected Poems*, I have chosen poems that seem both to have lasted well, and to illustrate Brasch's growth as a poet who still speaks, I believe, to younger generations of readers.

Brasch was born in Dunedin in 1909 and died there in 1973. With Allen Curnow, Denis Glover, A.R.D. Fairburn and R.A.K. Mason, he was one of the writers whose work marked a 'rebirth' of New Zealand poetry in the 1940s. In 1947 he founded the pioneering literary magazine *Landfall*, which he edited for twenty years. He was a generous patron of the arts and artists, but he valued poetry above all, even if in one mature poem he described his own work as 'A handful of verse uncertain in shape and style' – this from the magisterial editor whose approval so many sought.

As he wrote later in his memoir, *Indirections*, his father, who wanted him to follow a business career, scorned his ambition to be a poet, saying, "'If you're a poet, you must have a message. What's your message?" Silence. "You haven't got a message! All right. Then you can't be a poet.'" In retaliation, Brasch became determined not to succeed at whatever his father expected of him, failing to do well at Oxford and – more briefly – at Hallenstein's, the family firm. His *Journals* reveal, however, how he struggled for years first to believe in himself as a poet, then to find an occupation that might secure him a place in postwar New Zealand.

He may have had no 'message', but he did have subjects: loss, for instance, his mother having died when he was four years old, and the Otago landscapes where he grew up. His first poems were printed in the Waitaki Boys' High School magazine, and in 1929 his work appeared in *The Oxford Outlook* alongside his contemporaries Stephen Spender and Louis MacNeice. His models were the poems of Keats, Shelley, Wordsworth and the early Yeats, but as his own harshest critic, he recalled later 'the prevailing cloudiness of my ideas and aspirations, the vagueness of my similes and metaphors (Shelley and water, Keats and water, sometimes Yeats and water, but mostly water)' (*Indirections*, p. 151).

*

With face turned always to the sea …

Brasch's first collection, *The Land and the People*, printed in 1939 by Denis Glover at the Caxton Press, gave promise of what he might one day achieve. In eight of its twenty-one poems, New Zealand was his subject; he focused more sharply on landscape and the natural world in 'Waianakarua' and 'Pipikariti', and in the opening lines of the title sequence, 'The Land and the People':

> With face turned always to the sea, where night
> Rises and day is overcome,
> What expectancy or dream,
> Mountains, holds your inward sight?

The poem's last couplet foreshadows a theme in later poems such as 'The Ruins', in *The Estate*, that of a future hidden in the past:

> Yet sometimes memory stirs in them
> And leaning forward into time
> They see the root become the flower.

'Waianakarua', dedicated to the sister of his Waitaki school friend Ian Milner, is the first of Brasch's many poems addressing his extended family of friends and other writers, often taking the form of 'letter' poems in which he explores questions of place and identity.

*

… distance looks our way …

Brasch's second collection, *Disputed Ground: Poems 1939–45*, appeared from Glover's Caxton Press in 1948. Its title spoke both of wartime Britain and Europe and of his own internal struggles: would his conscience allow him to become a pacifist, like some of his friends, or should he enlist – and in which service? Having decided to enlist, he failed the medical examination and became a fire-watcher, spending terrifying nights on roof-tops during the Blitz. In July 1941 he began work as a translator at the Intelligence centre of Bletchley Park, and later with the Foreign Office in London. The sensitivity of these activities saw him place a thirty-year embargo on his personal papers, preventing his journals from being published until now.

Little of Brasch's wartime experience as described in *Indirections* can be seen in *Disputed Ground*. After several years of struggling to write on a range of subjects, he came to accept that 'it is only when I write of NZ, directly or indirectly, that I am given rein' (*Journal*, 30 August 1943). In 'Forerunners', he recognises the earlier Polynesian inhabitants of New Zealand who 'named the bays and islands'. The language may seem quaintly Romantic today, but it announces the themes of later poems:

> Behind our quickness, our shallow occupation of the easier
> Landscape, their unprotesting memory
> Mildly hovers, surrounding us with perspective,
> Offering soil for our rootless behaviour.

Brasch had ambitions for a large-scale ode on a similar theme, but ironically his most successful poem from these years, 'my first real poem', as he perceptively called it, was a sonnet starting 'Always, in these islands'. In its final form, it would lose its Audenesque second quatrain. Thanks to Brasch's sharp observation and evocative images such as 'from their haunted bay/ The godwits vanish towards another summer', and 'distance looks our way', this poem was widely quoted and anthologised. Nevertheless, it would be twenty years before Brasch himself would feel completely satisfied with it.

Only when Brasch saw his poems included in Curnow's important *Book of New Zealand Verse 1923–1945* did he begin to feel some confidence in his abilities. As he wrote in his journal for 31 August 1945, 'the fact of being well represented gives me a great sense of support, of being established, having arrived – it is public recognition, & I may now be able to call myself a writer without blushing, & be able to face the family as an independent being.'

*

I walk among my great-grandfather's trees …

That new confidence is obvious in his next collection, *The Estate* (1957). Since his return to Dunedin in 1946, he had worked with Glover and Curnow and others to launch the quarterly journal *Landfall*. As editor, he had ensured that it was soundly established, thanks to the support of the Caxton Press and to his own private income, which allowed him to work without pay and meet contributors and other writers elsewhere.

He dedicated the title poem, a sequence of thirty-four sections, to T.H. (Harry) Scott, an early contributor to *Landfall* whom Brasch had come to know on his visits to Christchurch to see the periodical through the press. Its verse paragraphs of flexible five-stress lines, interspersed with musical and varied lyrics, enable Brasch to explore and discuss his own re-awakening to New Zealand's landscapes and weathers, and to celebrate the lives and work of friends such as Scott, painter Colin McCahon and composer Douglas Lilburn.

The Estate reveals him making himself at home in his own country, as if for the first time. Now he is an established poet with important work to do – even if he does lament, in one poem addressed to James Bertram, that 'we are plainer, sadder, more wary, perhaps more alone.'

In middle life when the skin slackens …

James Bertram noted in his valuable study of Brasch (1976) that in his fourth collection, *Ambulando* (1964), his poetic style was changing, becoming 'a good deal more compressed, incisive, and vigorous … a more human voice …' In poems such as 'Ben Rudd', with its subject a reclusive farmer on the hills above Dunedin, and 'Cry Mercy', he speaks more directly to his reader than ever before:

> Getting older, I grow more personal,
> Like more, dislike more
> And more intensely than ever …
>
> Unloving and wanting love,
> Nearer to, farther from
> My cross-grained fellow mortals,
> On my level days I cry mercy …

Being 'Unloving and wanting love' was a continual torment for Brasch, as he reveals in his diary: 'Why this perverse persistent longing for happiness – actually for the companionship of marriage & children? for someone to share the world with? I ought to know well enough by now that I find most of my happiness when I'm alone; that I'm not fit company for anyone for long & soon chafe to be on my own' (Journal, 18 February 1958; Hocken MS-0996-009/025).

Brasch did indeed, however, form strong attachments, for instance to Harry Scott. The sequence 'In Your Presence' in *Ambulando*, coyly subtitled 'a song cycle', is clearly love poetry. But he neither identifies the object of his affection, nor makes it clear whether his love is reciprocated. Poignantly, in his diary for the following year he quotes Auden's couplet, 'If equal affection cannot be, Let the more loving one be me.'

A genuinely missing no-man

Not Far Off (1969) was Brasch's largest collection, reflecting his new-found freedom after what he called the 'twenty years hard' of editing *Landfall*. His style continues to develop, with echoes of the bitter later Yeats in 'Chantecler', of Robert Graves, and – unexpectedly – of the East German poet Johannes Bobrowski, whose poems Brasch was reading in German as they came out in the 1960s, and whose 'voice' he echoed in his tribute poem 'Ode in Grey'.

'Signals' is unusual in that Brasch speaks frankly of physical sex, seemingly from experience and not just in longing, while the conversational piece 'Man Missing' worked well for the very private Brasch in his few public readings: 'the man writing this now/ Is gone as he makes his bow'. By contrast, 'At Pistol Point' is his resounding manifesto for the status of poets, whom 'it is forbidden to question':

> Questioning is the poet's business,
> Officially, of course, not personally;
> Poets are servants, not masters.
> Poems ask their own questions.
> Poems are questions put to you
> At pistol point. They ask your life.

When Brasch died in May 1973 he left a folder labelled 'Book 6'. It contained typed copies of eighteen poems together with the twenty-six that make up the sequence 'Home Ground'. In 1974 that would become the title of his sixth and final collection. He also left manuscript notebooks with the jottings and hand-written poems he worked on in hospital during his last illness, then at home in the few weeks that remained to him. As his literary executor, and after careful consideration and discussion with some of his close friends, I included a selection of them in *Home Ground* under the heading 'Last Poems'.

I bid you welcome to my house …

The poems assembled by Brasch himself for 'Book 6' are among his strongest. Some are conversational and direct, while others are gnomic and riddling. The title sequence reveals the mature poet at ease in his home town of Dunedin, able at last to welcome 'Friends, though I do not know you all' to 'blow in continually/ With every season'.

I took a liberty in publishing these 'last poems', which were not of course authorised by Brasch, who could work on poems for years before he believed they were fit to publish. But even as hand-written first drafts they demonstrate an immediacy, a truth to their occasion, that speaks of their maker as he faces his own mortality:

> Farewell the careless days.
> Now I enter another rule
> Laboriously piecing together
> The hard grammar of dependence.

Despite the cancer that was taking his life, Brasch shows little of self-pity in these poems, writing one to the younger poet Peter Olds, who was a patient in the same hospital; one to Janet Frame, who had herself endured hospitalisation; and one last perfect gift of a lyric, 'Winter Anemones':

> The ruby and amethyst eyes of anemones
> Glow through me, fiercer than stars.
> Flambeaux of earth, their dyes
> From age-lost generations burn
> Black soil, branches and mosses into light
> That does not fail, though winter grip the rocks
> To adamant. See, they come now
> To lamp me through inscrutable dusk
> And down the catacombs of death.

Editorial Notes

Charles Brasch's complete published poetry can be found in his *Collected Poems* (Oxford University Press, 1984).

Biographical notes on people associated with poems in Brasch's first two collections can be found in the 'Dramatis personae' appendix to *Charles Brasch Journals, 1938–1945*, (Dunedin: Otago University Press, 2013).

Brasch appended notes to a few of his poems when they were first published. I have included these, as well as my own notes to others of his poems, as footnotes.

Abbreviations used in footnotes

Ind   Charles Brasch, *Indirections: A Memoir 1909–1947*
            (Wellington: Oxford University Press, 1980)
Bertram   James Bertram, *Charles Brasch* (Wellington: Oxford
            University Press, 1976)

Acknowledgements

I should like to thank the following people and institutions for their help and advice in various ways: the Librarian and staff of the Hocken Collections, University of Otago; Max Gimblett; Wendy Harrex; Jocelyn Harris; Donald Kerr; Peter Olds; Max Richards; Pat Roddick; and Margaret Scott.

Alan Roddick

POEMS

Man of Words[*]

I am a citizen of the English language,
Home that I carry with me all homeless days,
The sole country that will not convict me
Of race religion politics financial status,
Allowing mere life, consenting I am that I am,
A man of earth, suckling of time and place
And word, loosed to the freedom of the word-hoard.

I dwell here in my knotted history
Where I am every man who runed or knitted
The words that wear me and recite my story
Among the countless sagas of the word-kin;
I descend the purgatorial days to darkness
Unbreached, to forgotten souls time would not pity;
I live the thoughts of men their words remember.

I bear my thought alive in words that live me,
Thought that was breath in other times and orders
Of words not mine my forebears lived and traced
Across the barbed earth and by its waters;
I marry tongues, eras and lives, living
Them in these words I trace in dust and leave
For others in their day to bear and live.

---

[*] This late poem was among typescripts in Brasch's papers after his death. It was
published first in the *Collected Poems* (1984).

From THE LAND AND THE PEOPLE AND
OTHER POEMS (1939)

The Land and the People (I)

With face turned always to the sea, where night
Rises and day is overcome,
What expectancy or dream,
Mountains, holds your inward sight?

Do you remember through this plausible day
The maternal nightly flood
Where all things rest and are renewed
And separateness falls away?

For all your creatures have knowledge of that greater sea,
But born and dying to the sound
Of water on these shores and wind
They are governed by the momently

Event, and put from mind that disturbing power.
Yet sometimes memory stirs in them
And leaning forward into time
They see the root become the flower.

Pipikariti*

Stone weapons, flint, obsidian,
Weed and waveworn shell and bone
Lie in mellowing sand with wood
Of wrecked ships and forests dead.
Winds confuse the sand and soil,
Long-rooted grass and sea-fed pool
Contend between the cliff and sea
That creep close for fiercer play –
The caress of earth and water
Stretched together till they shatter
Impetuous side against stiff side
One silent and one loud.
The sweet sun and the wind's light stroke
Charm that fury into smoke
And music, twirling the blue spray
And lighting rage with a fierce joy,
That of the wasting strife appear
Only a lulling ghost of war
Intoning in a measured chant
The history of a continent.

---

*   'Pipikariti' is Brasch's spelling of Pipikaretu, a beach on the seaward side of the
    Otago Peninsula; see *Ind* 18.

Waianakarua

(For W.)*

Tall where trains draw up to rest, the gum-trees
Sift an off-sea wind, arching
Rippled cornland and the startling far blue waves.
Westward the shapeless low hills are forced
Here by a twisting amber stream,
Still in one pool under the corner willows
And crossed by the stone bridge beside the mill.

Knowledge ends thus with the traveller's glimpse;
But there imagination wakes
Vivid with an alternative creation
But near-related, complementary,
Later attainable; and flashing
Unknown visions of the known,
Rivals that time's tenderness shall reconcile.

And so, pensive in the still train, I follow
Your footsteps on the flying tussock
And through the dry manuka thickets,
And feel your heart warm to the hilltop winds
Won by sea-tales and a mild despair;
With you pierce the underbrow caves, forcing the creepers,
And rest in the grey untouched light, listening,
Hearing the fall of years
Soft and swift as the fall of leaves
One-voiced and even as over stones the stream.
Then into time I follow, as you ride
Circling at your shoulder or far
Watching your path through seasons, lives,
Or singly, or by dark –
Watch, but nothing here of you
Speaks the inexpressive face

The rough skin of your country.
                              Only the thorn
Alone on the parched rise, inhuman matakauri
Dry-green and fibrous, sorrowing,
The gum-trees that offer their flower, their sweet fruit
Lightly to the bright and dangerous wind,
These only eloquent
Here at the entrance to your country stir
Among the falling years that drift my eyes;
Until the recollected train
Moves on, past the landmarks, past the fallen years,
The passing land, the lives.

---

*   The dedication is to Winsome Milner (*Ind* 81, etc), daughter of the rector of
Waitaki Boys' High School in Oamaru.
Line 32, 'matakauri': the modern spelling is matagouri.

The Land and the People (III)

There are no dead in this land,
No personal sweetness in its earth;
Mountain and forest stand
Solemn and dumb as the forever
Stars, untouched by the sheep's path,
The climbing hand upon the rock
Loverlike, or the watching lover
Humble from far off. And the newcomer heart,
Needing slow-paced generations, the shock
Of recognition after long heedlessness,
Routine and ripening memory,
To make of new air, new earth, part
Of its own rhythm and impetus,
Moves gauchely still, half alien.
Only in the wash of time
Identifying, as the sea
Isolates, can earth and man
Into understanding grow
And to a common instinct come.
Not the conquest and the taming
Can make this earth ours, and compel
Here our acceptance. Dearest dust and shadow
Must we offer still, becoming
Richer as our loss falls home
Into her safer present keeping, who
Compounds our ash with the trees' blood,
The living and the dead inseparable.

Crossing the Straits

You that nightly cross the straits,
For whom a darkened island waits
To start with daybreak up from sea
Actual, proven; whom the wet quay
And shunned grey streets conduct to some
Transforming oracular rite; and whom
The city at last silences
And drowns, unwilling to set eyes
Upon its victims, after breaking
Every promise spoken, or speaking
In false smiling; – you that crossed,
Burning, in the silent post-
haste ferry: what great promise hung
Above the dark island, what tongue
Uttered out of night what word,
To draw like a migrating bird
You fearless over?
                           For no light
Can pup those promises of night,
Substance, and creature; no, nor give
Yesterday's wantless world alive
Again, nor pass across the straits
You, whom no darkened island waits.

From **DISPUTED GROUND:**
POEMS 1939–45 (1948)

Forerunners

Not by us was the unrecorded stillness
Broken, and in their monumental dawn
The rocks, the leaves unveiled;
Those who were before us trod first the soil

And named the bays and mountains; while round them
    spread
The indefinable currents of the human,
That still about their chosen places
Trouble the poignant air.

But their touch was light; warm in their hearts holding
The land's image, they had no need to impress themselves
Like conquerors, scarring it with vain memorials.
They had no fear of being forgotten.

In the face of our different coming they retreated,
But without panic, not disturbing the imprint
Of their living upon the air, which continued
To speak of them to the rocks and the sombre, guarded lakes.

The earth holds them
As the mountains hold the shadows by day
In their powerful repose, only betrayed by a lingering
Twilight in the hooded ravines.

Behind our quickness, our shallow occupation of the easier
Landscape, their unprotesting memory
Mildly hovers, surrounding us with perspective,
Offering soil for our rootless behaviour.

The Islands (2)*

Always, in these islands, meeting and parting
Shake us, making tremulous the salt-rimmed air;
Divided, many-tongued, the sea is waiting,
Bird and fish visit us and come no more.
Remindingly beside the quays the white
Ships lie smoking; and from their haunted bay
The godwits vanish towards another summer.
Everywhere in light and calm the murmuring
Shadow of departure; distance looks our way;
And none knows where he will lie down at night.

---

* See *Ind* 343. This is Brasch's final revision of the poem, which he settled on some
  twenty years after its first publication.

A View of Rangitoto[*]

Harshness of gorse darkens the yellow cliff-edge,
And scarlet-flowered trees lean out to drop
Their shadows on the bay below, searching

The water for an image always broken
Between the inward and returning swells.
Farther, beyond the rocks, cuffed by pert waves

Launches tug at their moorings; and in the channel
Yachts that sprint elegantly down the breeze
And earnest liners driving for the north.

Finally, holding all eyes, the long-limbed mountain
Dark on the waves, sunk in a stone composure;
From each far cape the easy flanks lift

In slow unison, purposeful all their rising length,
To meet and lock together faultlessly,
Clasping the notched, worn crater-cone between them.

That cup of fire, drooped like an ageing head,
Is fed with dew now and a paler brightness;
For the rushing anger sank down ages past,

Sank far beneath the sea-bed, leaving only
A useless throat that time gradually stopped
And sealed at last with smoky lichen-skin.

But the mountain still lives out that fiercer life
Beneath its husk of darkness; blind to the age
Scuttling by it over shiftless waters,

The cold beams that wake upon its headlands
To usher night-dazed ships. For it belongs to
A world of fire before the rocks and waters.

---

*   See *Ind* 179.

Otago Landscapes*

1 On Mt Iron

Red sun, remember
The waterless hills,
Glare of light in
The water-courses.

No milk of cloud
Shall be offered you
From these dried breasts,
To your bronze heaven
No pitying tears.

Thin-skinned the mountains,
And the rocks stained
With crepuscular lichen;
No sap in the thorn,
No voice among shadows.

Red sun, remember
The earth lost in
A shudder of heat.

2 Karitane

Sea-flower, seaweed, shell.
Hollow bells of the sea
Ringing, ringing
For the red sea-anemone

Swaying over the rock,
For the grasses tall as waves
That bow and sing to the wind,
And the black keep of pines
Where day its sweetness stores,
That, loosened, loads
The strewn, shaken airs.
Brimming poppies nod,
Clematis twines
Closer in to the basking wall.
On the tall platform under the flag
Laughing girls climb
To take the air and gaze,
And over the sea's breast
Peering through blown hair
Feel their breath come faster,
Launching into the wind
Thoughts that sigh and swell
With amber tresses of the sea,
Drawn to the green caves under
The fluted wave,
To the singing among the rocks,
The echo in the twilit shell
Of distant bells and muted thunder.

3 Henley on Taieri

Sullen, the stream gives no clear image back
To the black swan,
Scarcely answers the even, rippling wind
Or press of cloud, but slides
Noiseless in umber coils, eluding
The light that patters on the willow leaves
And flares from the white flanks of the hotel.

Friendless river,
Furtive, scentless,
From gorge to gorge over the yielding plain
Thirstily thrusting;
Saying no word to
Manuka or briar rose
Green bough or golden,
But sidelong, alien,
Onward swirled
Beyond leaves and faces,
No duct of life but
Cold seeker
Of self-dissolution
In the bitter and formless
Light-engulfing
Pit of the desolate sea.

*   For Mt Iron, see *Ind* 95; for Karitane, *Ind* 3.

Great Sea[*]

Kona Coast, Hawaii

Speak for us, great sea.

Speak in the night, compelling
The frozen heart to hear,
The memoried to forget.
O speak, until your voice
Possess the night, and bless
The separate and fearful;
Under folded darkness
All the lost unite –
Each to each discovered,
Vowed and wrought by your voice
And in your life, that holds
And penetrates our life:
You from whom we rose,
In whom our power lives on.

All night, all night till dawn
Speak for us, great sea.

August 1939

---

* See *Ind* 347

Soldier in Reverie

The world is single in his sight. He sees
Nothing he would have willed, nothing to content him;
Yet as he gazes it seems the fruit of his will,
Of his and many wills, many a deed and longing.
All its fragments are held together in his eyes
Through one long moment without regret or desire;
All its lives have meaning – though not that which they sought,
For their achievement is failure, and on each of them lies
The shadow of what they refused and was taken from them;
Purpose glimmers through its blind proliferation,
He perceives in its wildernesses the waters of kindness,
And there, O there he would live and plant his devotion.
He gazes: the world is single and whole; for him
Pardoned, justified, redeemed, and loved.
But in that very instant the world unwitting
Shatters the singleness he alone had given it,
Recalling him to his forgotten place
Among its multitudes whose role is anonymity,
Plunging his word of life in its incoherence.

In Memory of Robin Hyde 1906–39*

He could not win you easily, your death,
Though always hovering near.
Two wars he took for instrument, and that last
Cup of frustration; then he closed and struck
In the sour attic above the summer square,
And you were his and glad to be possessed.

In houses by the sea, through wounded China,
You tempted him defiantly.
Sometimes in conversation we could feel him
Near you, no enemy then, for you would turn,
As though asking for aid, to catch his eye
And hold him in obedience to your will.

By choice you stood always on disputed ground,
At the utmost edge of life,
Gazing into the firepit of disintegration
Whose lavas threaten our small inherited fields,
Whose poisoned fumes and ash of disbelief
Unnerve the quick blood and becloud our vision.

And there about you disease, hysteria, despair
Gathered their monstrous forces,
Corrupting our paper strength, that freely drained
From all we longed for still and still affirmed;
Yet you would not turn away to happiness
In distance and memory where life can be refined.

So they destroyed you. They were stronger. They triumph,
Commanding, unmanning us now.
It is their year; harvests of the hapless fall

Before them in Europe, as Gertler here, and Toller
Overtaken at Central Park. Nor shall we know
If those who follow us can put down their rule.

You were an adversary they had to master:
We shall see none to confound them
With blacker courage. Nor shall it be for blame
To have fallen to their power. Only the mightiest
Can really destroy, the darkness they command
Is utter, and their kiss a final calm.

London, December 1939

---

*   See *Ind* 345.

From THE ESTATE AND OTHER POEMS (1957)

Blueskin Bay

Ngaio and broadleaf people the grassy coast
Of green hills bent to the water
That stirs, hardly stirs in the wide arms of the bay,
Fingering the rocks lightly, for a season of calm
Laid asleep in its iron bed
Under the circling air, the dome of light.

Softly the fields descend, from knolls of grass
Down into dazed water,
Out of silent air into the sea's silence,
Out of the hovering laughter of light
Into a world of downward-darkening mirrors
Where sea creatures coil among irresolute shades.

Watching, erect in light, the headlands keep
Day's limpid triumph
Over ocean solitudes,
In swanlike calm above the crests of snow;
The white gull is master of the air
And trees untroubled dream beside their shadows.

They stand in windless time on the hill's breast,
Green broadleaf, ngaio casting its twilight flowers
Out of the leaves' arbour into emerald day;
They descend the cool paddocks, where horned roots cling
And plunge beneath the soil,
Down the steep turf that bares its scalp, until
About them rises the ocean circlet of rock
And the drifting waters they go down to meet.

In Memory of Willi Fels (1858–1946)*

Shaping in a garden for fifty seasons
The strong slow lives of plants, the rare and homely,
Into an order sought by the imagination,
    A precinct green and calm

Where climates, continents, civilizations mingled
And for a leaf-framed listening Apollo
The bellbird lingered over its flawless phrases,
    He watched a distracted world

And studied in all things to draw men and peoples
Together, that each should learn the others' ripest
Wisest creations, and, by beauty persuaded,
    Cold envy, false fear forget.

Oh not that human folly, inhuman hatred,
Be covered up, or discounted, or forgiven;
But that in each the best be discerned as truest,
    The final expressive form

In which it is most itself, and speaks most clearly
To those who would hear, as he, the quick and eager,
Everywhere sought and heard. Yet he was never
    One to delight alone,

But loved to take others with him into the shining
Weather of joy, where understanding transfigures
The meanest features, and strangers are strangers no longer,
    For all life breathes as one.

Far-seeing, of the sturdy lineage of the reconcilers
He came; and while his kind continues, calmly
And quietly active, earth shall not lack sweetness,
    Nor the human cause be lost.

---

*   Willi Fels was Brasch's maternal grandfather.

The Ruins

I have seen them still and clear in the bareness of dawn,
Strong hulls of shadow by no sunlight feigned.
I have watched them troubling the wind, rooted, opaque.
Air was about them; a dead leaf from their ivies
Rustling freed itself and fell coldly;
Trees kept their settled distance, grasses,
These grasses I touch now,
Knelt softly against the bruised face of the stone,
And birds in early wide-eyed flight
Skirted them as though making their constant passage.
Yet there is nothing here, nothing but the grasses
Of a level space open to the sea's quiet.

Can it be that what is to come is already here –
That the preparations are made, and what they point to
By some happy conjunction
May grow visible and seem even now to be?
That the air makes advances, drawing on the future
For these ripe clairvoyant moments, to load
Some artless plot of earth with burdens
That time lays up for it, and that the mind
Inexplicably sharpened may perceive
Through the loud deliverances of sense
Other shapes and workings, the undreamed of issue
Of currents unmarked or misconstrued?

But it is seldom that time opens unguarded
Or that I am able to see,
For if I look and wait there is only the careless now.
So this mild afternoon
The level space lies innocent, no walls
Lift up serpent wreaths of ivies
That bind their stones in a knot of death,

The wind flows unparted
Where I shall always see them cleaving it,
And sinks into the distance, or turns away
Into another era,
And is lost, lost in the sea's quiet.

Oreti Beach

To Ruth Dallas[*]

Thunder of waves out of the dying west,
Thunder of time that overtakes our day;
Evening islands founder, gold sand turns grey
In ocean darkness where we walk possessed.

What does it mean, this clamorous fall of night
Upon the heart's stillness? What pledge can they give,
These passionate powers of the world, that we might live
More surely than by the soul's solitary light?

---

[*] Ruth Dallas (1919–2008) was a poet and novelist and a close friend and associate of Brasch's.

To J.B. at Forty[*]

Twenty-five years, dear J., have gone over our heads
Since we discovered each other's worlds and could say,
Life begins here, as we spun the ardent hours away,
Or lying after lights out in dormitory beds
Wondered at what we were then. And what are we today?

We thought earth ours, all the future ours – it seemed
That time had never spelt such hope before;
What we would do with our lives we could not tell, but were sure
That men would listen to us and that all we did or dreamed
Must persuade the world. Can we be sure any more?

What is there now to be sure of, after these years
Of man's betrayal by man, amid this slow
Crumbling of every human certainty, till men have no
Power except for doom that darkens even the spheres,
And all we dare hope is somehow to endure and grow.

But our true faith was in one another, the heart's
Election, and that remains when all else is gone;
Though we are plainer, sadder, more wary, perhaps more alone,
Though we must go on playing our disenchanted parts,
That first love lies too deep for us ever to disown.

Yet I was false sometimes to what I knew
And loved; alas – alas, I have betrayed
Your dear image too often, and guilty and dismayed
Find no self-forgiveness, remembering how you
Taught me the magnanimity of the free and unafraid.

To myself I seem more shadow than substance, one
Who slipped through life and found no living-space
Except in his friends' love and the momentary grace
Of real identity they lent him who had none,
Perpetually dissolving into time and place,

A handful of verse uncertain in shape and style
The only evidence for his existence;
But you – I see you always in the sunlit distance
Declaring like a landmark in face of men's denial
Waters that run pure with life's serene persistence.

---

*   The dedication is to James Bertram (1910–1993), journalist, writer, academic and life-long friend of Brasch's; see *Ind* 84, etc.

54

Letter from Thurlby Domain[*]

To Colin Newbury

I walk among my great-grandfather's trees.
Through poplar and pine pour the steady seas
Of mild mountain wind, norwester, in long-
Breathed tide and calm of voice shaking their strong
Rock-bedded roots; yet, below, the air is still
In this orchard-harbour deep embayed in the hill-
Terrace, where cattle graze in thick grass
By pear-tree, apricot, walnut, and through the ground-bass
Swell of the wind quivers and rings a thread
Of song from leaf-lost birds. But dumb and dead
In this quick summer stir the old house decays,
Hollow, unroofed, with staring window-bays
And boards torn up; from fallen foundations the stone
Walls lean outward; garrulous starlings own
It as home now, but after ninety years
No man any more.

         When a long-lived house disappears,
Ruined, into this raw-man's-land, and grows
New harvests of elder and thistle and briar rose,
An air of contentment breathes from it, almost
Of reconciliation, the laying of a ghost –
That figure of brute man breaking in on nature,
Defiling its sanctities, altering rhythm and feature,
That represents us all, that haunts all
Our works till they too are proved natural
By their decay, and so are lost to us
And given back to nature; like this house.

A debt is paid here then, a silent wrong
Atoned in silence, and one man's works belong
At last to earth. But man's earth: is it not now
Man's, marked with the sign of axe and plough,
Watered, shaded, settled? For men have brought
Ripe gifts to soften the rigours that contort
This towering snow-dazzled sun-shot world
Of rock on rock, mountain on mountain hurled,
Cupping cold lakes, bare valleys curved for sleep.
Look, he who built here planted: road, hedge, and sweep
Of fields, garden and stable; this avenue
All summer sounding, cool in the blazing blue,
Its poplar-fountains soaring from some green well
Under the waste where there was nothing to tell
Of water's sweetness; and hill of twilight pine,
And the wind-censing gum's tattered ensign
Over the running grasses; ash, acacia,
Lime, and tall towers of wellingtonia –
All his; and he in Lebanon plucked the cone
From which that masterful cedar sprang alone;
He, my great-grandfather whom I did not know,
Who built and sowed and left his seed to grow
Cradling the land. So these rich groves (and those
That crown now the bare peninsula he chose
For Queenstown Park) make him a monument,
And marry us to this earth; but for the spent,
The sober house, that held so mildly together
Brunswick and Lincolnshire in colonial tether –
All trace of person gone, all family pride,
Call it man's first-fruits offered and not denied.

Cast on this Eden we must violate still,
Where shall we find that good for which we do ill
By necessity, but so long? Where, if not in
The heart's peace from which all worlds begin,

Our wrong and loss and pain with a due kiss
Sealed in acknowledgment of our genesis;
Not by inflaming nor by stilling desire,
But learning in the fire the nature of fire,
Upon the wheel replenishing the wheel,
Caught in the dance that sifts unreal from real.

Dead house and living trees and we that live
To make our peace on earth and become native
In place and time, in life and death: how should
We entertain any other goal or good
Than this, than here?
                        From Crown to Coronet
The sun has swung overhead, and burning yet
Thirsts for western waters; the wind will soon die
In the trees; at my foot a lizard slides among dry
Stalks and is gone with a flickering goodbye.

---

*   For Thurlby, see *Ind* 39. The dedicatee is the historian Colin Newbury, born in
     Dunedin (1929), who studied at the University of Otago.

Autumn, Thurlby Domain

What news for man in a broken house, old trees
And ruined garden dying among the hills?
Nothing is here to distract or to surprise,
Nothing except the plainness of stone walls
And trunks unleafing, what has been planted and grows,
What has been built to stand; that now fails,
Having served its time,
And goes back ripe to the earth from which it came.

What news? Are old age and decay so new
They put us out of countenance, offend
Lives that have long forgotten how to grow
And die, and do not care to understand
The elemental language of sickle and plough,
Of nursery and orchard, sun and wind,
That speak to us everywhere
With the same untroubled intimacy as here?

What we have found before we shall find again,
No new thing; age and youth seem strange to us
Who can no longer relight the morning sun,
Bring each day to birth in that bitter stress
And eddying joy that mark the life of a man
As years ring a tree; only in loss,
All knowledge stripped away,
We stumble towards our naked identity.

All civilisations, all societies,
Die with a dying house. These walls beheld
Rites of birth, marriage and death, customary days
Of equable happiness, dear hope unfulfilled,
Heart practised in patience and hand grown wise;
All human glory men have dreamed or hailed

Lived here in embryo or
Epitome, and dies in character.

What ceremony does autumn hold this afternoon
With green-gold bough and golden spire – what rite
Of pirouetting poplar-dancers, to crown
The dying year, the death of man's estate,
With brilliance so raptly and so lightly worn?
In celebration of death we consummate
Our vows to place and time,
In sickness and in health to live and die with them.

Self to Self

'Out of this thoughtless, formless, swarming life
What can I find of form and thought to live by,
What can I take that will make my song news?'

'Where nothing is, a seed may yet be sown.
Does not chaos cry for the forming hand?
Thought and form be the new song you choose.'

'But if this outward chaos only mirrors
Chaos within, confusion at the heart,
How can I start, where settle to begin?'

'The formless and the thoughtless then your theme;
Knowing disorder like the palm of your hand,
Set up house there, amid the stench and din,

And be at home in your own darkness, naming
Hand and mouth first, wall and ceiling, then all
That hurts you or offends, without as within,

All that you hate, that maddens, that merely is –
The ants, the dumb oxen, the golden calves
(For there is nothing you have the right to refuse);

And when you have bent before them, made them one
With the waste heart, they will obey your word,
Out of disorder bring you song for news.'

'To work in what I fear, subject my weakness
To power, surrender speech for an idiot dumbness? –
O worse than death, the very self to abuse.'

'What have you left to lose, disorder's own?
Only from incarnation of disorder
Can order spring, and you must end to begin,
If you would sing you must become news.'

Fuchsia Excorticata

In dry green shade the terracotta bark,
Loose-papered, glows like sunburnt skin,
A peasant's, but of finer texture, clearer hue,
Warm Etruscan;
Dark leaves with pale under-side, pointed, bladed,
Composing their own shadow and privacy,
Will not be flattered by the most royal sun
Into momentary brilliance not theirs by nature,
But close and secretive
Observe an earthen plainness averted from light,
And brief in the wind move without grace.

Long ago the fuchsias forgot birds, seasons, weather,
Old forest play and talk,
Turned from all fellowship outside the tribe;
And now the last lingering sweetness of their sap
Breaks unnoticed in slight crisp flower-bells
Alert with honey, scattered along the boughs
And rifled quickly by fantail, wax-eye, tui,
In the shade of indifferent leaves.

An ancient taciturn breed, squat and sunless
On hillsides foaming beneath windy light,
They draw from earth an aboriginal blood
Begotten under midnight and no moon
To spells their darkness broods over and breathes,
A sap with black dew nightly replenished.

Rest on the Flight into Egypt

After this hour, no other? Who can say;
Is not each hour eternity? The winged herald appeared,
Appears for ever; and other eternities, maybe,
Gather about garden and hill, awaiting their time.
Do not ask. All that is needful now
You will find here; Egypt is far ahead,
And those high clouds, this open uninsistent stillness
Shut out Herod's servants.

Listen, the sea below falling in a clear bay
Has dropped its voice, and no
Echo out of time touches their resting place.
Only at intervals a sleeping wind
Sighs above in the cave of macrocarpas,
As if to lull the wide-eyed child
Who sees without watching as Joseph gathers sticks
Or a leisurely gull, silent, oars overhead.
And the mother holds him lightly, half smiling, half aware
Of mermaid grass springing fresh among rocks
Ancient with silvered lichens, and of the air
Of late afternoon that, free and flowing on
From hill to hill, lapping the farthest headlands,
Gathers height and valley and distant township
And farm and bay below
And insect trawler crossing plains of sea
Into one picture and one world with her
Who has no world
Except the infant at her breast, husband beside her;
They having no knowledge beyond hers
Nor other care than hers,
Living the one look and thought all share.

Yet wait: for a full hour unnoticed,
Downhill, past the fields laid out
With sheep or horses under the even afternoon,
Where a farm-house shelters among huddling trees
Pressed flat by the wind, there you can trace
A tiny barking of dogs, and cowman calling,
Just at the picture's edge. They have not heard
Of mother and child and the necessity
That brought this halt upon the winding hillside
Watched by trees and stones. And yet they too
Belong within the picture; they are that memory
Where each event finds place, where all that's acted,
Suffered, thought, enters, being strained through time;
Which they receive whether they sleep or wake,
Which they must harbour in safest ignorance.

Rain over Mitimiti Mountains

A grey stole of weather drawn from sky to sea,
White-furred with mist trailing on mountain ledges;
The clouded harbour breathes lightly as rain.
A horseman slowly passing lifts his hand
In silent greeting, but does not pause or turn.
Beneath the infinite whorls of Whiria Pa Hill
Pipi-gatherers stray about the wet shore.

From THE ESTATE

*To T.H. Scott**

ii
Cool kingdom of wind and cloud†
Moored between tropic fire and polar dark:
Leaf and rock
Sea-shaken in the dawn,
Mountains older than time's brood –
All, all in their generations shudder and are gone.

Here too lodge, board,
Son of man, breaking the stone field
To found a world,
Raising shadow walls
For multitude and solitude
And in memory and forgetfulness of all souls.

Middle earth of heart's home,
House of dust cradled in roaring air,
By water or fire
Watch, wait with us
That through all the weathers of time
We may balance our pride against our nothingness.

---

*   T.H. (Harry) Scott (1918–1960) was an experimental psychologist at the
    University of Auckland, mountaineer, an important contributor to *Landfall* in its
    early years and close friend of Brasch's.

†   'I have borrowed a line here from Hermann Hesse's poem *Süden*: "Kühles Reich
    der Wolken und der Winde". [Brasch's own note to this poem.]

iii‡

I think of your generation as the youngest
That has found itself, has seen its way in the shadows
Of this disconsolate age, this country indifferent
To all but the common round, hostile to every
Personal light men would live by. You may not be many,
You that have groped through the stifling dust of existence
And found water – you, shall I say, of the promise,
Scattered, one here and one there, the length of these islands;
To yourselves fumbling, fallible, often bewildered,
Oftener discouraged, your lives strewn with disorder,
And weak, and alone; yet to me as to others the lanterns
We look to, certain stars in a cloudy twilight,
More precious because of your weakness, because you stand single.
I count with you chiefly that painter, contracted to pity,
Who first laid bare in its offended harshness
The act of our life in this land, expressed the perpetual
Crucifixion of man by man that each must answer,
Rendered in naked light the land's nakedness
That no one before had seen or seeing dared to
Publish – an outrage to all whose comfort trembles
Hollow against such vision of light upon darkness.
And he who meditates under the green escarpments
That bound Wanganui, out of his rank rough acres
Constructing a garden, not in retreat, not escaping
Our time's turmoil, but better to focus in quiet
The shrunken image of man; intangible labour
With no clear issue, that yet for a whole generation
May serve to cleanse and sweeten the muddied life-stream
Of trivial daily existence. They too who are planting

---

‡ James Bertram (Bertram, 26), identifies the people referred to in this section
as 'the painter Colin McCahon ...; Noel Ginn, a fellow pacifist with [T.H.]
Scott now working in a plant-nursery; the writer G.R. Gilbert and his wife,
picturesquely attempting to plant vine and olive in Central Otago; [and] the
composer Douglas Lilburn'.

Deep in desert Otago Athenian olive,
Virgilian vine, pledges perhaps of a future
Milder and sweeter to mellow blunt hard natures
Of farmer and rabbiter, driver, storekeeper, orchardman,
With usage of wine and oil from grove and vineyard
Shading stony terraces, naked gorges
Scourged now by frost and fire, no human country.
And that forced listener to the virgin-moded
Tongues of these airy latitudes – grave or smiling
He listens, watchful, bow-strung to attention
Between our human talk and that world-tremor,
Half heard, he conjures into rites of music.
Others will follow; already you can hear them
Rousing, beginning, lighter because they venture
Where some have gone before and marked boldly
A possible way – for you still doubtfully possible,
Demanding all you possess of calm and courage
And edged intellect, and that warmth of spirit
Rarer than beauty – like genius a gift and equivocal.

iv
Dreaming that I am far from home, I come at dawn
To a white gate under a macrocarpa, giant-grown
Over its shaded paddock of worn and cropped grass
That swelling and curving outward dips, falls into space –
Bare scroll of sky, bare sea, that end-of-the-world sea
Nuzzling our rocks, the rocks of earth. And it is day,
Look, the white gate opens on crystal, on crests of fire
That glow, that hover; and in the stillness I can hear
(As light invokes hillside and town and river-bed
And models boulder and tree out of anonymous shade)
A new wind far off waking in tussock and bed of thorns,
And magpie's water-music among the parched stones.

vii

Green is the apple garden
And deep the summer shade
For dreaming or day-dreaming –
Lay down, lay down your head.

Here all earth's harvests ripen
With apple and with rose,
Dead ages and their wisdom
A trance of time restores;

And we, as in recollection,
Rise in our walled demesne
To act the world's unfolding,
Dance out the dream of man.

xi

What are we then that speak and turn to silence
When the oracular heart answers our question
With its dark saying echoed in every silence?

Side by side we listened to one another
As trees in wind listen, rooted dumbly
Although their branches signal from one to another.

We drank life from life as the spring wind mounted
And carried us through a strange masque of seasons
Far into landscapes of being no word had mounted,

Where we have been borne apart, yet speak over ocean
Silence, and answer question with echoing question
That haunts the hollow waste of the heart's ocean.

xii

Noon. In the campanile's narrowed shadow,
Before our eyes the dazzle of the laguna
And in the air its murmuring obbligato,
We lay and rested, gazing outward, upward,
And speaking fell into silence. High above us
In that white calm that breathed from all things living
The campanile soared in motionless bird-flight
Far beyond day, disclosing fathomless heavens,
Abysses of warm sky deeper than darkness,
Clearer than light, that seemed a vaster ocean
Where foundering time had cast its woeful treasure
As the ripe centuries sank in quiet, purged of
Their bitterness, an ocean free for entry,
Its trembling threshold limned in lightest outline
At the arrow's mark of the campanile, visible
Or hidden as lucent vapours flowed and parted
Admitting me or excluding, intent watcher
Lost to myself, lost even to Torcello's
Millennial stones and waters waiting on me
With all their past now in my meagre present
And drawing all my life into their stillness.
So for a moment under the wheeling tower
I dreamed, or woke; and bear that waking with me
Across the years, as then I bore these islands
Sleeping, and you unthought of, and all the future,
And those I shall meet for the first time tomorrow.

xiii

Do not ask tall Justice for the gifts of Love.
Justice parts, apportions; Love can only add,
Ignoring place and time and number,
All to nothing, all to all.

Justice never known in heaven was conceived
By our fallen nature, leaden deputy
For that restoring, that enchanted
Fount whose life it is to flow.

xiv
Waking by night as often I lie in stillness
And feel the hollow dark listening, troubled
As though some far-off note of dread possessed it;
And straining, holding my breath in the suddenly fearful
House, at length half hear, half feel continuous
The fall of winter seas assaulting, racking
This rooted earth and us.
                            Not longest summers
Can end the icy vigil of those waters
Circling the thunderous poles, or still their anguish,
That like a frost striking the helpless midnight
Steals upon earth. So all night through till morning
I hear that fathomless ocean breaking about us
In sleep, and all things borne to dissolution.

xviii
We who judge by results from moment to moment,
Counting success by number and notoriety,
Influence, place, what do we know of the life of
Growth, that darkness in which our being's heart-timber
Adds in the winding year
One slender ring – dense, true, of crystal fibre –
To its tried tissue? Changing, but from no centre
Of trust and knowledge, we reflect changes of weather,
But what strength have we to stand in this age of withering
Storm, to bear and survive?

I think of one who stood, our world's apprentice,[*]
In silence learning to grow; who, proud and impatient,
Stripped her will of ambition either to alter
Man's living or colour his thought, from her high garden
Studied a landscape for years.
She had sought early, a gardener by nature,
The lives of metropolitan yard and tenement
That, starved of soil for soul and body, might answer
Her care, putting forth leaves, becoming established,
Human with blossom and fruit.
And later on a hillside, with one companion,
She planted different seed, the unaccountable
Unseasonable word, that in its summer
And winter too bore richly, proving all weathers
Salutary to growth.
But finally alone, grieving and ageing,
All she had cherished lost to her, and troubled
In that most desolate thing, her faith, she practised
A winter obscurity where every season
Struck cold into her heart.
Yet in that winter there came, fluttering towards her
One by one, hesitant in their uncertainly
Straining youth, a dispersion, a murmuration
Of spirits drawn by her wind-flung word and offering
Homage, asking for strength;
Who formed a faint galaxy far about her,
A star-garden sprung in the waste nullity
To offer her concern a new employment
With talents needier than she had imagined
Nature could ever be,
Strong wilful wildings thirsty for direction

---

[*]   Brasch had in mind poet Ursula Bethell (see *Ind* 301, etc). 'Towards the end of
her life, Ursula Bethell quoted in a letter to me the phrase of "an English mystic"
which seemed to be much in her mind: "Faith is a desolate thing."' [Brasch's note
to this section.]

None can give; but she opened her life and gave them
Entry, as free as children to gaze and wonder,
And shared her thought with them and heard unwearied
Their preluding notes for a life.
And bent her way again to the resolving
Grave, all loss; a leaf in that unnumbered
Forest where dead and living never parted
Yield life to life through the mountainous ages
And the wind blows and is still.

xx
Fall till day's end fall,
Warm light, upon the mountain wall
Unclouded over summer waters, in air of down.

Day's dying, be long
And calm as these waters' lulling-song,
So we die with you into sleep when we lie down.

Day that can never end
And never dying light, O lend
For all our lives long this life you have called down.

xxiv
What have you seen on the summits, the peaks that plunge their
Icy heads into space? What draws you trembling
To blind altars of rock where man cannot linger
Even in death, where body grows light, and vision
Ranging those uninhabitable stations
Dazzled and emulous among the rage of summoning
Shadows and clouds, may lead you in an instant
Out from all footing? What thread of music, what word in
That frozen silence that drowns the noise of our living?

What is life, you answer,
But to extend life, press its limits farther
Into the uncolonized nothing we must prey on
For every hard-won thought, all new creation
Of stone bronze music words; only at life's limit
Can man reach through necessity and custom
And move self by self into the province
Of that unrealized nature that awaits him,
His own to enter. But there are none to guide him
Across the threshold, interpret the saying of perilous
Music or word struck from that quivering climate,
Whose white inquisitors in close attendance
Are pain and madness and annihilation.

xxx
Thistle, briar, thorn:
Dark sayings of an earth
Austere even in the joy
That gave them birth.

Sweet across snow, over rock,
Singing briar that sows
Mountain and desert with alms
Of poverty's rose;

Outlaw thistle, quick
Through wild and ploughed to run
With barbed defiant crest
Bowing to none;

And thorn, weaving in air
Thirsty nets of pain,
Pointed with seed-pearl flowers'
Compassionate rain –

How shall I read your tongue's
Gnomic economy,
To whom the muse of silence
Made the word free?

Be my companions still
With wind and star and stone
Till in your desert music
I hear my own.

xxxii
White star on the mountain ridge
Soaring slow out of night,
Dance in the heavens for pledge
Of undefeated light.

Mark in the calendar
This night that now is day,
This dawning of the year
In darkness fallen away

Before a hovering star;
We shall not fear the night
Nor the remorseless year
Who walk by clear starlight.

xxxiv
Mountain midsummer; the sun's bright burning-glass
Hovering westward over the peaks of the Darrans,
High yet in heaven; the snow-touched airs still;
And we warm in our glade under rough mossed beeches
And frail-haired webs of lichen bleaching with age,
The lake silent, white the eastern passes.
We lie content at day's end, labour's end,
Quiet for thought or sleep; what can speech tell us

Here where all communication is
By silence, or by look or sign, or is given
As out of the motionless forest a small cry comes
Distantly, the soft rainbird's, that seems to echo
Some thought we could never utter, never frame;
Or sailing from high rocks above the bushline
A harpy troop of keas scatter and scream
Grotesquely, and we must laugh at their heavy antics
Over the forest depths where nothing stirs.
What more can speech tell than with raucous vowels
They hurl in missile messages from rock
To rock across the gorges; we study silence,
Ask understanding; words may be hindrance or help,
Illumination or darkness, at best can offer
An eye for us to see through; are never goal,
But bridge or station, as now when I must use them
To express what we have been, what understood
Without them.

    Day by day on this summer journey
We enter mountain kingdoms, watchfully thread
Ocean mazes of forest, scale the passes,
Yield to the valleys; and everywhere we note
In molten or marble torrent, in trees vaulting
Vast ruined courts of space rent from the sky,
In deer surprised on innocent lawns and plunging
Deep into forest gloom no ripple marks,
Or soundless mountain bells and lilies shaken
And cool everlastings wakeful under eaves
Of moss or shadowed by blind uprearing sphinxes –
In all, an unknown life breaks on our life
One moment, and is withdrawn; a life we hardly
Suspect, so near, yet so remotely still,
Fast in its gathered and suspended power.
And yet how often even in our own lives
Do we – stumbling towards death in blind impatience –

Live from the pure spring of life, the stream
That feeding all action flows beneath unhurried;
Now in a dream, now in an aimless pause
At evening, or overheard through the gales of autumn,
Speaking to us in a language we have not cared
To learn, and we are caught up, troubled, reminded,
And feel its current throbbing far, far beyond
The shallows of our day.

What can we look for
But understanding, what reality find
But life – life burning in us: *omnia lassant*
*praeter intellegere.** And we are vowed –
You on your path as I on mine – to that learning,
Going a common journey by diverse ways,
That here, this night of summer, the rocks our witness,
Has led us to such calm: we have no life now
To earn, for we are life's; singly, divided
Without isolation; at one in drawing breath
With all that breathes.

Clear through dusk the waters
Fall in the forest; now the first dews come
With the first star: stillness: and unextinguished
The peaks float, dark in the transparent west.
Can we preserve till morning, for many a morning,
Making it ours through day and night and year,
This strength, this ripeness of heart by all earth's powers
Confirmed, by crystal air, transfiguring snow,
All that we know, all that we are, unfading?

Dunedin–Christchurch 1948–52

---

* Brasch's own note read, in part: '*Omnia lassant, praeter intellegere* [Everything
tires, except understanding]. This saying [is] attributed to Virgil.'

From **AMBULANDO** (1964)

Ambulando*

i
In middle life when the skin slackens
Its loving clasp of our loose volumes,
When the bone tree stiffens and its well-jointed branches
Begin to creak, to droop a little,
May the spirit hold out no longer for
Old impossible terms, demanding
Rent-free futures where all, all is ripeness,
But cry pax to its equivocal nature and stretch
At ease with wry destiny,
Supple as wind bowing in every reed.

ii
Now that the young with interest no longer
Look on me as one of themselves
Whom they might wish to know or to touch,
Seeing merely another sapless greyhead,
The passport of that disguise conducts me
Through any company unquestioned,
In cool freedom to come and go
With mode and movement, wave and wind.

iii
Communicate with stones, trees, water
If you must vent a heart too full.
Who will hear you now, your words falling
As foreign as bird-tongue
On ears attuned to different vibrations?
Trees, water, stones:
Let these answer a gaze contemplative
Of all things that flow out from them
And back to enter them again.

iv

I do not know the shape of the world.
I cannot set boundaries to experience.
I know it may open out, enlarged suddenly,
In any direction, to unpredictable distance,
Subverting climate and cosmography,
And carrying me far from tried moorings
So that I see myself no more
Under some familiar guise
Resting static as in a photograph,
Nor move as I supposed I was moving
From fixed point to point;
But rock outwards like the last stars that signal
At the frontiers of light,
Fleeing the centre without destination.

---

*   Brasch said the title was his 'dog-Latin for "going places"'.

From Ben Rudd[*]

1

High above the town
He lodged with wind and sun
In a hollow of the hill
Whose tussock arms fell
About him, streams ran by
Low-voiced night and day.

Narrow hut and black hearth
Crouching to earth,
Billy, bunk and crude
Bench, axe and spade,
Candle and shotgun –
And the flag of green
Outside by the mud wall,
Potato patch and full-
Fruited raspberry, gooseberry.

2

No one crossed his door,
No one crossed his path
For fear
Of sudden threat or oath.

And yet his single care
Was to keep at bay
All who might interfere
Coming to pry –

The righteous who would trick
Him to their lawless town
And hold him lost and weak
To waste among men

Far from hill and sky;
So, helpless to run,
When words were thrown away
He seized his gun.

4
Start alone, end alone.

All known faces gone
And familiar talk done;
Heart that poised on a knife edge
Eased now of stubborn rage,
Beyond fear and hope content
Not to ask, not to want,
Free to live its own days
Wasting no breath upon the ways
Of other men, but every thought
Bent to work the sum out
Of what is and what is not.

7
Moving higher at length
He left field and wall behind,
Looking down at them, looking beyond them
To town and harbour, and farther yet
Swart-green headlands, white beaches
And the sombre arc of ocean
Unheard except on still nights after storm,
But always present, the oncoming night
Waiting, the end of time waiting;
Cold ocean, grave of waters
And world's burial ground.

8

Few passed his door,
None crossed his mind.
At home to summer air
And railing wind
He lived out day and night
As though none but he
Trod earth's deck, beset
By sea and sky.

10

They found him when his strength failed,
Carried him down at last
Tired beyond protesting.
And the town received him,
Nursed him barely a week,
Until death shook
His leaf from the bough,
Out of then, into now.

From In Your Presence

a song cycle

I practise to believe,
And work towards love.
How should I see
Until I study with your eye?

Nothing I know
Unless you answer for me now.
What was I made for
Except to write your signature?

*

Far and far away,
Scent of a rose in the wind,
Your voice comes over the wires,

Smoke of mountain fires –
But you and no other, you,
Clear in the drift of day.

And oh, the heart's play,
Exulting of waters loosed,
As word with word conspires.

*

I read your signature
In the rose and in the rock and in the fabling sea,
And follow through every when and where
The lines of your face and the print of your hand.
Yet write for me sharper on eye and ear
Your form and name, my living bread,
That I may never go hungry more,

But even in the farthest galleries of air
Wake and sleep as though in your hand.

*

Morepork, shrewd sentry owl,
Watching night pass,
Sleepless, censorial,
Never heed us;

We have love's work to do,
We shall not stir
While your grave star-show
Turns in the air;

Driving the world round
We, by our rites,
Burnish your darkness and
Fuel those lights.

*

Buddleia for its scent in August,
Honey barb stinging the dusk,
I prize, and for that fume of anguish
Your love lends it, your severing love.

White cold star splitting the dusk,
Sweetness that searches nerve and soul
With blade of ice, and you, descended,
Stabbing my heart with lightning love.

*

I rove, you stay,
Each constant in our own way,
Revolving in the erratic circles we must
Trace from dust to dust.

Faithful, faithless,
What do such counters mean to us who confess
That each draws for life-blood the whole
Breath of the other's soul.

*

Light at your window:
I come from the dark to find you,
And go again into the dark
With you for lantern.

May your light burn
Every long night for me,
And in that night without end
Where last I must seek you.

Seventeen April[*]

This was your day
For all the years that life wound us together,
Day of remembering, day of forgetting,
When the sun rose to dry childish tears,
Confirming for autumn and winter weather
The arched world and the home of day
That could not fall
Because you kept all years and kept our play.

This was your day
All your years long, eighty-eight times together,
Day of renewing, day of fulfilling
As child, grandchild, greatgrandchild hears
Wind-word, laughs in sun-god's weather,
Regents for you of the world's day
Although there fall
Shadow on shadow to darken all your play.

This is your day
And shall be, all my years together,
Day of recalling, day of reconciling,
Whatever be the world's fears
And the face of fortune's or season's weather,
Until the life you found this day
And lived out, fall
From me too passing on in endless play.

---

[*]   This was the birthday of Brasch's grandfather, Willi Fels.

By That Sea*

Cold I lay you beside that bitter sea
Where men have laid their dead since the first flight
From Eden and its everlasting day,
In ground where young grief cast her lot;
No foreign soil to you, who have tried before
The sill of exodus, the farewell shore.

I lay you in the common grave of man
On a bed of earth and under a blanket of stones
To sleep man's sleep in quiet and be gone
With him, leaving no trace among rocks and thorns
But your seed of dust that we tread underfoot
To rebuild the falling mountains, nourish the root.

I take no leave by these waters that turn and return,
Salving grief in their monotony.
You live with me in your death as though reborn,
As if I had not learned, till you came to die,
That in our last role reversing our first one
We must play to the end father and son.

* The subject here is Brasch's father, Henry Brash (see *Ind* 9, etc).

Cry Mercy

Getting older, I grow more personal,
Like more, dislike more
And more intensely than ever –
People, customs, the state,
The ghastly status quo,
And myself, black-hearted crow
In the canting off-white feathers.

Long ago I lost sight of
That famous objectivity,
That classic, godlike calm
For which the wise subdue
Their poisonous hot hearts,
Strength of arm and righteous
Tongue, right indignation.

To know all, to bear all
Quietly, without protest,
To bend never breaking,
To live on, live for another
Day, an equable morning –
Is that what men are born for?
Is that best of all?

To each his own way,
For each his particular end.
Judging one another
By inner, private lights
Fortuitous as ourselves,
We leave some other to judge
By impersonal sunlight

Objective, as we hope,
In the after-world, if any,
What we have made of ourselves,
How we have laid out
That miserly talent, gift
Bestowed on us at the start
For the problematical journey.

How shall I make excuse
That I am not with those
Who lost the loving word
In sumps of fear and hate,
Convicts, displaced persons,
Castaways even of hope?
On them too a sun rises:

Any of us may be hunted
Among them any day.
What certainties assure
Another dawn will wake me
Or the galaxy swim on?
To live is to remember
Remembering to forget.

I lay down no law
For myself or my neighbour.
I search for can and must
Along the broken flare-path,
Pitching left and right
Shaken by voices and thunders,
By other lights, by looms
Of chaos, and my self-shadow.

Liking and disliking,
Unloving and wanting love,

Nearer to, farther from
My cross-grained fellow mortals,
On my level days I cry mercy
And on my lofty days give thanks
For the bewildering rough party.

From NOT FAR OFF (1969)

A Closed Book

The worm that lives in darkness
Raised his head to me
Swaying whitely as he spoke:
– Why do you invade my kingdom
With your murderous light?
Here I live for ever
Threading the leaves of a closed book,
Harming none that do not see,
Ignorant of you till now as you of me.
I know you mean my death, and I
Have no defence; kill if you must
My life intolerable to you,
But do not think you destroy then
A life earth holds of no account,
Empty, profitless; it is your own,
The same life-stream bears us both,
Bearing the memory of countless lives,
Some we know, some not know,
All carried within our blood.
Kinsman, farewell:
Strike, and remember.

I would have answered, but
A voice of air was saying:
   I am that memory, I speak for both,
One who kills, one to be killed.
When necessities conflict
Nothing can reconcile them
Except a death that marries them
By separation

In a world too small for two.
Meeting now, you turn away,
One dead, one living,
He who kills forfeiting the life
Of him he kills.
World is one in grief for two
That you do not know.
Bow your head and raise your head
Going as you must,
You who are one in me.

The world swam in dust
Before my raised hand.

Lady Engine*

The Lady Engine steamed across the road.
Quietly, black-shining.

Pavement, hedges, houses
Drew back to give her way
Through afternoon, no one about.

Slowly passing, she looked at me,
Not turning her head.
Grave, kindly, silent. Looking.
I gazed back. We gazed at each other.
Nothing said.

What did we feel, Lady Engine?
Only felt; no words. Gazing.
Gazing took our breath.

Gazing till she drew away,
Not looking now.
I followed with my look.
Past the hedges, past the houses,
Out of day.

        Gone. Vanished.

No sound, no smoke in air, no rails crossing the road,
No sign of stain anywhere.
Houses, hedges, pavement, all as before.

Gone, gone.
        Where?
            No where?

Here or
Therewhere –
Lady Engine:

Under the world.

---

*   See *Ind* 12.

Ode in Grey

(In memoriam Johannes Bobrowski, 1917–1965)[*]

Well for you to die
Not living in vain, poet
Never born, because living
Always, even as dead
And now newly dead;
Voice of oldest earth
In its leaping freshets, in the pulse
Of its night pores,
Heart-voice of human kind,
Gong, echo, time-bell
Of one man and all men;
You of Memel waters,
River town and forest town,
You of marshes, reed-beds,
Soliloquies of sky and plain,
The lost tongues and silent peoples
Of once Sarmatia;
You may die well.

Yes, for itself
Your earth grew you, our
Still human world,
Joyful still, fertile
In all its morts, maimings –
In what seldom and dissembled
Rejoicing, in what anguish
Of horror and hope it bore you,
Your words tell, unknowing,
In vows given, not said.

You speak always
In that same even tone
Learned from the earth itself, from
Its braiding mists, ore veins silently working,
Listener tense-still,
You toll-tell your world,
Wind plains, rivers of starlight, forest, snow,
Ground voices of waters,
Crack of frozen branches
And men timelessly bearing, breaking,
The plough-work of the years,
The slow teeming earth
That mothers birds, animals, men:
So you weave again the wounded
Web of living.

Words cannot right old wrong.
You ask no forgiveness
For the death of peoples, annihilation,
For life trodden, beaten down
By armies, by informers,
Sepulchre judges, righteous clerks,
All who slice and parcel
And label and regiment
What is made one life
And given once only
To spring with the young birch bough
Into free air
Into unity of light –
Earth-life, strangled,
Earth itself poisoned:
There is no forgiveness.

But there is sleep still, is
Death sleep,
And there is memory,

Your work, poet;
You, one with all
Going forth by day, sunlit, to labour
In the footfall of men,
The beating of hands
And hearts calling out
Unwearied until sundown;
Returning nightly
With the homing, with
Those who fall by the way,
Those rustled into prison
Or snuffed out for ever and no print found;
One and all, your people
All one, world
And single life always,
Poet, your song of being.

No, you are not dead,
You do not lie down to die
Giving your body to earth.
You wake in the ears of men
When they cannot speak
To tell their truth out,
Waters under the ice
Witness to you, the bird that seals
Its flight with one last call,
The young leaf raising its arms
To light, the grey leaf
Coiling into dust –
All, all are your kin,
All speak your tongue.

---

*   Johannes Bobrowski was an East German poet whose work Brasch encountered
     late in life.

Man Missing

Someone else, I see,
Will be having the last word about me,
Friend, enemy, or lover
Or gimlet-eyed professor.
Each will think he is true
To the man he thinks he knew
Or knows, he thinks, from the book.
Each will say, Look!
Here he is, to the life,
On my hook or knife;
And each, no doubt, having caught me
Will deal with me plainly, shortly
And as justly as he can
With such a slippery no-man.

Well, I'll be quite curious,
Watching among the dubious
Dead, to see what they make
Of this antique: Genuine, or Fake?
Myself, I've hardly a clue;
I know how I feel, what I do,
But how true my feelings are
And why I perform a particular
Act is quite beyond me,
Analyse and prod me
As I will, as they will,
Nothing quite fills the bill;
And the man writing this now
Is gone as he makes his bow.

Gone, for I never can bind
My seesaw will or mind
That keeps changing with the weather,

Not only from bad to better
And back, but changing aim
And course, myself still the same,
And looking everywhere
I find no centre anywhere,
No real self, only a sort
Of unthought self-conscious thought;
A house with no one at home,
Where any visitor is welcome
To name, try, spare or pan
A genuinely missing no-man.

Open the Heart

To run a thousand miles from a thousand men,
Flinching from every face indifferent or hostile,

Masks you cannot compose a mask to meet –
Doesn't it still leave you where you started,

Heart pounding because you could not endure
To catch your face naked in the mirror

And see heart, face, the whole quivering self
No more than a puff of wind

Raising the dust, settling into dust – ?
No no no, that's mere

Decoration, rationalization, still running away –
Simply, you dare not stand, because

To speak out is more desperate than to keep silence,
To open the heart is to bleed to death surely.

Signals

No two bodies taste alike or smell alike.
Your cat will tell you so sooner than I can,
But not more certainly.

You are not what you were before we knew each other;
I cannot explain the difference, but
All my antennae report it.

Nor can I put my finger on the difference in myself
Now we have learned to answer signals
We did not receive once.

Your skin tastes and smells of tropics where I walked
Barefoot, nostrils wide and fingers
Winged over waves,

Where shadows drew me in through their like leafiness
That is yours now, leafy, woodier to taste
And salt with the salt we share insatiably,

Yours, mine, still distinguishable though mingled
As limbs are, as breathing is,
As tongues that taste each other.

At Pistol Point

It is forbidden to question poets.
Study their work and you will not need to.
Putting questions is not for you;
You have enough to do for life
Governing your heady clamours,
Reporting daily, filling in forms,
Keeping the lion statisticians fed.
Questioning is the poet's business,
Officially, of course, not personally;
Poets are servants, not masters.
Poems ask their own questions.
Poems are questions put to you
At pistol point. They ask your life.

Bonnet and Plume

I am going to survive you all.
Yes, I am going to be a survival.

I shall survive my wings, with the kiwi,
My third eye, like the tuatara,

And my enemies and my friends,
Those who speak to me and those who pass by.

I shall live in a different world;
It will be mine still, but not yours.

It will have survived you and gone on living,
You will be part of it without knowing,

You will have made it and stopped making,
I shall be making it until I drop

And leave it for others to leave to others
Until it survives them all, bone-naked.

From Chantecler

V

Never call me wise,
What's wisdom but white lies,
Pap for cowards and fools;
Call me cunning, quick
As the snap of a dry stick,
Breaker of locks and rules.

Never call me kind
Or good or of one mind;
I want no fancy name,
But to laugh in the sun and bed
With love, sing for my bread,
And play a losing game.

X

To folly, anger, lust and pride
I pray in my distress;
They do not turn a deaf ear
Nor does their power grow less,
Iron crutches that never fail,
Goads I curse and bless.

On love and pity once I leant,
But they were broken reeds
That would not spur me to stand up
Despite a heart that bleeds
And tear from fortune's laden arms
My unrepentant needs.

Pity will never heal the sick
Nor strike down the proud,
Love lift a mountain-moving hand

Where the poor go bowed –
But these that fan the despondent blood,
To them my life is vowed.

They keep me straight through crooked years
With rack and thumbscrew play,
They set tongues in my gaping mouth,
They give me words to say;
How should I know I was alive
Unless I felt their sway!

They lay my sorry talents out
Zealous to get and spend,
They lead this life that is called mine,
It is they affriend, offend,
Forging the good and ill name
That misshapes my black end.

xi
To hate your neighbour as yourself
Is mere self-preservation
Spreading the one-eyed, one-way force
Of hatred's self-destruction,
The self you can no longer
Look in your glass and worship
In wondering self-absorption.

To see your neighbour as yourself
His heart stripped self-naked
Is to confess in every heart
The hateful and the crooked
Beneath its lies and boasting,
And at the roots of hate
The trivial and vapid.

To shun your neighbour as yourself
Maddened with self-knowledge,
The vapid and the trivial
That bear no human message –
Destructiveness, forgiveness
Work to the one issue:
Let hatred wreak its outrage.

xii
Where I love I hate
And cannot
Love where I hate

But, blind in the net
Turn and burn and
Curse the foiled heart.

From **HOME GROUND** (1974)

Shoriken[*]

1
Feel the edge of the knife
Cautiously –
Ice-keen
It lies against your cheek
Your heart
Will pierce at once if you should stir
Yet offers
A pillow loving to your head
A sword to cross the malevolent sea.

2
The wood of the world harbours
Lamb and lion, hawk and dove.
A world of lions alone
Or a world of doves – would it
Capture our headstrong devotion
Harness the wolf-pack of energies
That unsparing we spendthrift
Earning our lives till death?
Where in its white or black would be work for love?

3
The merciless strike with swords
With words
With silences
They have as many faces as the clouds
As many ruses as the heart
The fountains of their mercy never run dry.

4
In a world of prisoners
Who dare call himself free?

5
Every mark on your body
Is a sign of my love.
Inscribed by the years, you tell
Unwittingly
How we travelled together
Parted and met again
Fell out sometimes, then made peace.
Crowsfoot, scar, tremulous eyelid
Are not matters for shame
But passages of the book
We have been writing together.

6
Giver, you strip me of your gifts
That I may love them better.

7
To remember yesterday and the day before
To look for tomorrow
To walk the invisible bridge of the world
As a tightrope, a sword edge.

8
What wages are due to you
Unprofitable servant?
You come asking for wages?
Fifty years long you have breathed
My air, drunk my sweet waters
And have not been cut down.
Is it not a boon, living?
Do not your easy days mark
The huge forbearance of earth?

9

The bluntest stones on the road will be singing
If you listen closely
Like lilies or larks
Those that may stone you to death after.

10

Rising and setting stars
Burn with the same intensity
But one glows for the world's dark
One whitens into tedious day.

11

All yours that you made mine
Is made yours again.

12

To speak in your own words in your own voice –
How easy it sounds and how hard it is
When nothing that is yours is yours alone

To walk singly yourself who are thousands
Through all that made and makes you day by day
To be and to be nothing, not to own

Not owned, but lightly on the sword edge keep
A dancer's figure – that is the wind's art
With you who are blood and water, wind and stone.

13

One place is not better than another
Only more familiar
Dearer or more hateful
No better, only nearer.

14

He is earth, dying to earth.
The charge of life spends itself
Wears, wears out.
His sole enemy is the self
That cannot do otherwise
Than live itself to death
            death
The desert sand
That dries all tears
            death
Our rest and end.

15

Selfless, you sign
Your words mine.

16

To cross the sea is to submit to the sea
Once venture out and you belong to it
All you know is the sea
All you are the sea
And that sword edge itself a wave-crest of the sea.

---

* Brasch's own note read: 'Shoriken is the Japanese name of one of the eight
  Taoist Immortals. A kakemono by Motonobu in the British Museum shows
  him crossing the sea, balanced on the edge of his sword.' Brasch owned a
  reproduction of this scroll (Bertram, 50); see also *Ind* 241.

Semblances*

1

He sits to read, smoking and considering.
His hand holding the cigarette is poised
Considering, his head held by its look
Balanced, a little inclined, all suspension,
Directed to the book his left hand holds.
That ruffled head was black once, now almost
Whitened, but his the same; his lips tremble
In concentration, as always; he will turn
Shortly to me and look the unspoken question
That lies between us in the cool air still.

2 Walking Invisible

To Frank Sargeson

I knew you first in that uniform of the rejected,
A work-tried, rain-coloured mackintosh
In which you walked invisible,
An image of every other man,
The misshapen streets; and failed to know you.
It seems now an emperor's new clothes
To show you naked as yourself, salt man.
And seems on any other man
To confer the dignity you lent,
Singling him out as one who makes no show
Of being other than that daily self
You touched once and made more precious.

---

* The first poem possibly depicts James Bertram.

Eternal Questions

*To Nicholas Zissermann**

Dostoevsky always wanted to settle them at once,
Before all else, in his boiling youth, those eternal questions,
That raged and tore at him and hurled him down.
But found that he must live them out for life,
Encountering them in every bedroom and kitchen,
Trivial and momentous one flesh –
Trunk and leaf, bark and sap of the single tree.

So they took root in him, cried in his hot voice,
Possessed the festering city that he haunted –
And made all cities one, speaking one language
Of common need implacable in man's beating blood.

Raskolnikov will not turn his burning eyes away
That splinter the concrete, blaze from the running gutter.

From every cynic street the sparks fly up, fly up.

They strike out of dull words, they breed in silences.

---

* Nicholas Zissermann (born 1911) taught at the University of Otago 1967–77.

World Without End

In all weathers? If imagination permit –
If imagination qualifies, then yes, in all.
Do you recall that day when the second war was ending
And from our sterile bureaux
We walked out into the green breath of the Park
Saying, 'Well, nothing more can happen now,
Nothing worse'? And it seemed so that day, that year.
How little we knew. There is always a worse and still worse
And no ending, though each in his turn is broken –
The will crumbled, the heart lost, mind given way,
And to humming hospital or knacker's yard
We are turned over, no longer master of our gates.
The end for each is no ending at all;
World persists, turning with us, in us,
Turned by us in all our weathers,
Intolerable to each, our common country.

'If Every Street'

If every street is called straight
How can you weave a winding path?

Like water, O like water
That always asks the lowest place.

To grow up straight as a tree
To spread arms wide like a tree

Exposing the breast and battered heart
Is to follow a tree's doom

Strung up first and then cut down
In tears, sweat, blood, water.

A straight street speaks for pride
Spare to the swift and the unready.

Round about roams the world
Lies down to a levelling wind.

Straight melts in the measuring eye
Stone to water, mortar dust.

The first man that fell from straight
Made length a crooked mile

Strewed milestones in star dark
By scent of water, light of leaf.

From Home Ground

i
Between the waves of sea and mountain
A drift of tide-wrack, mound of shells.

Blown about by winds. Buried in dust. Rain-sodden.
Baked by summers of sun.

Wind-shaken, moved. And moving, stirring within,
Alive. A hive, hive of cells, congregation.

Builded, self-begotten, self-willed.
Manhouse, man-made, a human city.

A company of men sailing through time,
Consignment of souls.

Between hills and waters, living,
On a planet whose heart of fire is dying down

In the assemblies of constellations,
The night host of the galaxies.

ii
City of nothing. Set under sky, beside waters,
Hill hollow. While tides move it lies unmoving
While stones rise and fall, wood dries to powder
In houses banks schools churches factories
While men tramp its streets from dawn to dawn after
And time flows over it and over its hill waves
And wears it like a falling rose the winds gather.

City of nowhere. Quivering, fast at the edge of the void.
See, its stones are water, its words dust, its people

Voices of ocean winds, wheels that turn in the void,
Gulls shrilling and vanished in air. In a trough between waves.
In the palm of a hand. A mound of shells, rose-petalled.
While smoking chimneys inscribe the clouds, while breath climbs
Into cloud, while blood thins out, fog, mizzle, sea-rain assembling.

Floats on the void edge. Past the sentry beat
Of breakers, beyond White Island, last step into nothing.
There in cavernous mists of dusk, icebergs prowl
The bottom sea, towering out of the night watches,
Warders of nothingness, brushing the noiseless stars that steer
By no earth-mark, courses set for that dark they trace
By their passage across the night, the tallest aerial masts.

Nowhere. Strewn over sea and sky. Torn in the gales.
Voices. Paper. Dust. Everywhere mingled, woven
Into the fabric, the seamless garment that all put on
At birth, that looses them dying. Everywhere. Of the fabric.
Here. World dreaming, suspiring. Nowhere but here
Which is everywhere. In the palm of a hand. A petal falling.
Stand and hear. Watch. All is, all here.

iii
I tramp my streets into recognition.
They know me now and make no sign, they keep
Silence for my step
Giving nothing away, but poker-faced
Enact their numbers
Dependable under sun and moon.
I can just run that gauntlet of stone lids,
Making my lips stone.

Do not betray, stiff
My streets, the pulsing inward of your port –
Great King, Filleul, London, Albany Steps –
Paling and crossed curtain, petrol station,
Blossoming plum, hospital, blood-red church:
Tell your frailties over to yourselves
As I retail mine,
Behind the advertised face, between fly
Mocking and despair.
I could not run the gauntlet of your tears.

iv
Friends, though I do not know you all,
I bid you welcome to my house.
Make it your own. Make me your own.
I had not guessed before you came
I might be ripe for such possession.
You must speak in my name now
And wear the mask that passes for me,
While I withdraw to play the host
Discreetly, keeping my doors open
And windows open to the sky
For visitors of all persuasions.
Let them blow in continually
With every season; I shall make ready
For all who come to make me theirs.

viii
I thought I had turned my back on examinations
When I came of age. Yet all my life since
Has been an undeclared examination
That does not fail to remind me day by day
Of the odds against me and the penalties
For inadequacy and unpreparedness
(No matter that one cannot prepare,
No matter that one is born inadequate),

And that will not finish until death grounds me
Without appeal, giving no second chance.

To sit any other test than this now
I have no patience.

I pray you pardon me;
Would stretch my tolerance to breaking point.

xi
I sit here silent and communicate
With the talking and the silent world
With all who pass in the chattering streets
Who dig drains and stand behind counters
Who teach sparrow children and run to catch
Flying numbers in ledgers
Who speak in parliaments who swing truncheons
And heave up paving stones and write on banners
Make Love Not War
All who are eating and drinking and dying
In hospital beds in reed huts
In planes crashing and waves crashing on rocks
All those performing birth committing marriage
And making love that brings others to birth
All who sit quiet and lie quiet in earth
And are the air we breathe –
I sit walk talk write love and hate with one and all
Writing in my book and watching in my glass
The day and night wind cloud and star
Footfalls and echoes in the street of time.

xiii
Before the light of evening can go out
The mountains have their features to compose,
The sea will commence its orisons,

And I must find a way
Among the indignant directions of the trees
Commanding to every compass point.

I ask the streets to guide me,
Past the shifty eyes of window-panes,
Beyond the forums and advertisements,

To some rough sketch of ground
Out of the traffic's ear
Where I may pitch a tent with plantain and pimpernel

Beneath the Pointers and the east wind,
And listen long to the night prowling
Over roof-skin and raw nerve-ends,

Unravelling the skeins that bind me
Into the world's close cocoon
To cover up my clamouring nakedness.

*

xiv
Silence will not let him go
Entirely; allowed a few notes
At the edge of dusk
He will be recalled before long
And folded into rock
Reassumed by the living stream.

xvi
I do not know what is permitted me
Speaking as I can
As necessity enjoins
Words wrung from the lips of silence
Night syllables

Waves of the sea ringing
For ever in time's ear.

xviii

I ask not to be confined again
By soil, by stones
In family plot or communal graveyard.
Do not leave my bones on the shelf of a catacomb
My ashes shut in a leaden urn
I have been cramped too long in this body
Too long the ward of a spirit
That could do little for it
Always commending, disapproving, correcting
Tedious school-mistress
Unable to control it or let it go;
A nice balance of frustrations.
Now I have done with all that
Schools and regulations
High chairs prisons poisoned shirts
Let me go free at last
Scattered on the winds
No name scratched on a stone behind me
I ask the world to be my grave.

xx

Dream of love, you only forsake us at last
In extremis. It is you after all
That bound us to life through the desolate years
When every personable figure had
Long since with reason turned to our juniors;
And yet you lingered encouragingly
And persuaded us that life held something still –
Just what, you would never be caught saying.
I look today at your final haunt, across
Crisp waters lightly stirring, and wonder,
Drowsily wonder beside the cabbage tree,

Grateful for everything, how I could have
Lived without you, missing the exaltation,
Deprived of the despair. If you deceive,
Blessed deception, that allows us to live
Beyond ourselves – powers, expectations
Working for us, though never our possession.

xxii

Right. At sixty, a man is dead, or as good as dead.
Left.　Just as dead as he thinks.
Right. He lives longer at his own risk
　　　　With no rights in life, nor claim to consideration –
Left.　Long past considering.
Right. He has burned his boats, buried his reticences –
Left.　His boats were his reticences.
Right. No need any longer to lower your voice
　　　　When speaking of him. No need to be tender about
　　　　His memory, his family, his good name;
　　　　You can say what you wish and not fear libel.
Left.　It would flatter him to be libelled.
Right. Why should he care what is said? He has done his
　　　　　　work,
　　　　His mark is made, or lost.
Left.　Made to be lost.
Right. He is only curious to see the image
　　　　Other people know him by –
Left.　The lust to be talked about.
Right. So he can put face and fashion behind him
　　　　And think of more immediate events,
　　　　Cloudlight and weather, his ebbing and flowing
　　　　　　blood,
　　　　The life of flowers –
Left.　And bills, and mistresses, and scapegrace children.
Right. That ask only consent and wonder,
　　　　Leaving no debts and no obituaries –
Left.　His debts are his obituaries.

xxiii

It is years now since I left the house
Where you keep looking for me still.
Day by day I change my custom,
Seldom sleep twice in the same bed.
Where I shall be tomorrow
And what face wearing
You might as well ask the wind.
You will find me only in yourself.

xxiv

Wind: displacement of air: liquefaction of forms.
The letters of the earth's book melted down
And every self dissolved to dust –
Dust that witnesses dissolution.

And then the air settles.

Leaves and houses reassume their bodies.

The alphabet is distilled out again.

xxv

In drab derelict marsh near the madhouse
Fenced off and cancelled as dead ground
The spur-winged plover steps and probes.
The swamp-pools and the reeds, brief sky, grant him circuit.
He gives no sign to heed the scorching traffic
Eat up the road that swings above his lifeland,
But stray nearby to watch and he will cry alarm
And run, distracting from his callow nest.
He lives, breeds, dies by instinct, nothing willed,
Habit-hovering in a stream of lives
Bent to the arc-flight of the seasons.
And yet, at moments habit cannot point,

Does he divine a consenting sky,
Consent of earth
To his necessity that is hers also?
Necessity, consent, slip through our fingers
That touch and lost the pulse of time.
It is he sustains the world, outside our care.

xxvi
The eyes of the world are looking through me
Unseeing
        or
At me, looking me over
In the slave market

Human eyes yet all
Of inhuman cold
That will not meet my eyes
Always measuring, seizing
Passing over, turning away

Leave no place in life
Allow no being

Close your eyes, world
For one night or day
To let me breathe
           breathe

My eyes will not close
Living –

From 'LAST POEMS'

Here too the leaf-dark forest bird
Calls from the pastures of the Dart
To cool at dawn night's long delirium,
Restore the mountains and the waters.[*]

From Night Cries, Wakari Hospital

Only the flawlessly beautiful
May be admitted to your presence;
To lift veiled eyes to yours
Perhaps to hear your voice
Even to approach and maybe
Kiss the hem of your garment.
Nothing of that for me
I know, I do not ask.
I do not even dream of it.
Enough that day and night from fabled birth to dying
I turn and turn
My ear to the wind
That mutters to itself bemused
Over and over without end
Fumbling with your secret name.

Tempora Mutantur[*]

Beautiful the strong man in his strength,
Happy the self-reliant.
I too rejoiced once
Walking the earth head high.

Farewell the careless days.
Now I enter another rule
Laboriously piecing together
The hard grammar of dependence.

---

[*]   *Tempora mutantur [et nos mutamur in illis]*, Times change [and we change in them] – Renaissance tag.

Fabled City of Agape

Fabled city of Agape, if you exist at all,
You are hidden deep in the wounds of life,
Among the wreckage, the blinding pain.

In different words long, long ago,
Before I was old enough to understand
You had spelt it out; and amazingly
My raw untutored heart remembered
And treasured you for those unforgettable words
And for your unknown name, Ferenczi.[*]

But only after forty errant years
Does the city rise and stand breathing before me;
Not in its walls, not in its rational laws,
But in that intangible inimitable air,
In the tender speech of eyes and hearts,
In loving-kindness of hands
Whose happiness is unwearying service;
The humblest of them in her own way a healer,
A glowing night-light, a day-flower friend,
Carrying unknown your unknown words.

It is the physician's love heals the patient.

---

[*] Hungarian psychoanalyst Sandor Ferenczi was a disciple of Freud's.

Watch-dog

Gnawing, gnawing the edge of night,
Black-barking dog,
You rend the seamless dark to tatters
The tent of sleep
That held me an oblivious hour.
Faithful guardian, would you destroy me?

A Word to Peter Olds*

Sleepless through long nights, I think of you
Hived in another cell of this same
House of pain and healing
And hope that you at least sleep darkly
Sealed fast from cries, lights, mechanized clamour.

Fellow, fellow-stranger, how can I reach you
By word or sign? We scarcely know each other.
We exchange a smile and greeting in the street
By chance, or in a packed interval at the Globe,
But too much seeming seems to separate us,

Years, custom, the habit of reserve.
Yet I think of you as one who goes
Up the mountain in shadow, where I would go,
Not knowing who I am, or why I must,
With yellow robe and begging bowl.

---

*   Peter Olds (born 1944) is a Dunedin poet.
The Globe Theatre, in London Street, Dunedin, was founded in 1961 by Rosalie
and Patric Carey.

Winter Anemones*

The ruby and amethyst eyes of anemones
Glow through me, fiercer than stars.
Flambeaux of earth, their dyes
From age-lost generations burn
Black soil, branches and mosses into light
That does not fail, though winter grip the rocks
To adamant. See, they come now
To lamp me through inscrutable dusk
And down the catacombs of death.

---

*   This poem was written by Brasch in hospital, after his friend Margaret Scott had
brought him a bunch of these flowers, just three weeks before his death.

From 'Back from Death'

1. Returning

You who caught me back from death
To the balefires of this breath,
Why did you not let me go
Out upon the midnight flow?

Did I ask to wear again
The hair shirt of a world of pain?
Did I ever ask for life,
The cry of love, the turning knife?

Not for us to ask, but bear
The wheel, the whirling fever-fair,
Not to question well or woe,
As we must to come and go.

Is there one who sees and cares
How murderously mankind fares?
Master of the silence, keep
Our question as we rage and weep.

4. With You

To Janet Frame[*]

Can you hear me, Whangaraparaoa?

Listen to your seas, listen to your tides,
To the moon pulling the deep.

I am there, under the waters,
In the winds, in the leaf that sighs.

I am there, sleeping in the rocks,
Under the houses, below the promontories.

I am the sea, I am the wind,
Everything and nothing, with you.

6. Titus Reading

He seems to smile
Because of the light on his face,
The light smiling on him
As he reads,
His father's smile,
His father's light.
But he reads, and does not smile,
As Rembrandt shows.

7
Silent the birds at morning
As raindrops shining on the leaves.

They have no autumn song,
Black shapes flitting through sodden branches.

They are bearing the year into winter,
Laying their stillness on our lips.

---

*   Novelist and poet Janet Frame (1924–2004) was living at the time on the
     Whangaparaoa Peninsula, north of Auckland.

The Clear*

It is all the sky
Looks down on this one spot,
All the mountains that gather
In these rough bleak small hills
To blow their great breath on me,
And the sea that glances in
With shining eye from his epic southern prairies;
Working together
Time-long
World's way.

---

*   'The Clear' is a local name for Prospect Park, in Dunedin, where there is now a
seat, and a plaque bearing the poem, installed in 2009 to mark the centenary of
Brasch's birth.

INDEX OF TITLES AND FIRST LINES